Angels Everywhere

Poems

Luci Shaw

PARACLETE PRESS
BREWSTER, MASSACHUSETTS

2022 First Printing

Angels Everywhere: Poems

Copyright © 2022 by Luci Shaw

ISBN 978-1-64060-720-0

The Iron Pen name and logo are trademarks of Paraclete Press.

Library of Congress Cataloging-in-Publication Data
Names: Shaw, Luci, author.
Title: Angels everywhere : poems / Luci Shaw.
Description: Brewster, Massachusetts : Iron Pen/Paraclete Press, [2022] | Summary: "Poetry written as if a heavenly being is darting in and out of viewing, bringing brief revelatory messages from somewhere beyond"-- Provided by publisher.
Identifiers: LCCN 2021053565 (print) | LCCN 2021053566 (ebook) | ISBN 9781640607200 (trade paperback) | ISBN 9781640607217 (epub) | ISBN 9781640607224 (pdf)
Subjects: BISAC: POETRY / Subjects & Themes / Inspirational & Religious | LCGFT: Poetry.
Classification: LCC PS3569.H384 A82 2022 (print) | LCC PS3569.H384 (ebook) | DDC 811/.54--dc23/eng/20211029
LC record available at https://lccn.loc.gov/2021053565
LC ebook record available at https://lccn.loc.gov/2021053566

10 9 8 7 6 5 4 3 2 1

All rights reserved. No portion of this book may be reproduced, stored in an electronic retrieval system, or transmitted in any form or by any means—electronic, mechanical, photocopy, recording, or any other—except for brief quotations in printed reviews, without the prior permission of the publisher.

Published by Paraclete Press
Brewster, Massachusetts
www.paracletepress.com

Digitally printed

Praise for ANGELS EVERYWHERE

"Luci Shaw crowns a lifetime of poetry with angels literally everywhere in her shining lines. She demonstrates a holy attention. For her, she says, the writing of these poems is 'like knitting smoke.' For us, however, this 'smoke lifts / like a scarf for an angel.'"

—PAUL J. WILLIS, author of *Somewhere to Follow*

"In this book, more daringly than ever before, Luci is 'enabled to investigate/ the underside of the obvious.' She concludes that even during the pandemic, 'we are joined in love, never alone.'"

—JEANNE MURRAY WALKER, author of *The Geography of Memory*

"Luci Shaw has faithfully plowed the field of words for more than a half-century, planting and nurturing gardens to nourish us. The poet is 'blindsided by / the beauty of blossoms' and she considers how to 'turn / back in time… / re-inscribing it / fresh…with/ a vivid spectrum of color.' This is precisely what we need—to look up again, and glimpse hope."

—BRUCE HERMAN, Lothlórien Distinguished Chair in Fine Arts, Gordon College

"Every reader of Luci Shaw's work knows there are, indeed, angels everywhere. She is an incarnational writer and these new poems are rooted in the flesh. This is not a book of memory, but a book of living fully in the present, trusting in the unknowable, and always moving towards what is radiant, even if such going forth comes at a cost."

—ROBERT CORDING, author of *Only So Far: Poems*

"Luci Shaw's poems are messengers from a greater world. She catches a wide range of light—from small glass shards to larger pieces glancing from the sun. 'I want birds to fly / in and out of my poems,' she says. Shaw captures our longing for flight during our captivity to the pandemic. Thank goodness for these power lines."

—DIANE GLANCY, author of *Home is the Road: Wandering the Land, Shaping the Spirit*

"Luci Shaw opens wide this world's windows to honest contemplation and contagious hope. Most importantly, Shaw teaches us 'to move the air of . . . thinking,' making space for vision and grace. In a world brimming with both beauty and pestilence, each poem is a tiny baptism."

    —**MARJORIE MADDOX**, author of *Begin with a Question*

"'The poet's job is elemental,' writes Luci Shaw. 'Notice. And make notes.' Clearly Shaw takes her own advice and has noticed that angels are everywhere. We can be grateful for her gift for noticing as we read this latest volume by our most prolific poet of faith."

    —**MARK JARMAN**, author of *The Heronry* and *Dailiness*

"In the material world we too often take for granted, eternal verities open up at the poet's attention. For Luci Shaw, each event, each circumstance says its own angelic name everywhere inside the name of God."

    —**JEANINE HATHAWAY**, author of *Long After Lauds*

"Luci Shaw reminds us that angels are messengers from another world and that they can be found everywhere, especially in the concrete Here and Now. Her poetry translates these messages for us through the formal brilliance of their language. Each of these exquisite poems is an Annunciation."

    —**GREGORY WOLFE**, author of *Beauty Will Save the World*

"Shaw is, as ever, eager to translate the testimonies of all things great and small, from the behemoth to a bud on a chestnut bough. Seizing upon searing encounters in nature that she calls 'little revelations,' she opens occasions of transcendence. Her clear-eyed faith kindles within me a longing 'to drink wind free as wine.'"

    —**JEFFREY OVERSTREET**, author of *Auralia's Colors* and *Through a Screen Darkly*

For some of the angels in my life:
Jennie, Claudia, Deb, Laurie, Doreen

Also by Luci Shaw

POETRY

Listen to the Green
The Secret Trees
Postcard from the Shore
Polishing the Petoskey Stone
Writing the River
The Angles of Light
The Green Earth
Waterlines
What the Light Was Like
Harvesting Fog
Scape
Eye of the Beholder
The Generosity

FOR CHILDREN

The Genesis of It All
The O in Hope

WITH MADELEINE L'ENGLE

Wintersong
A Prayerbook for Spiritual Friends
Friends for the Journey

NONFICTION

God in the Dark
Water My Soul
The Crime of Living Cautiously
Adventure of Ascent
The Thumbprint in the Clay

Contents

Foreword		7
	Angels Everywhere	11
Part I	**Out of Darkness**	
	Considerations	14
	Gaze	15
	Prey	16
	Bones	17
	The Sense of Language	18
	Embryo	19
	Questions in Time of Pestilence	20
	Persistence	22
	Voyage	23
	Diurnal	24
	Enabled	25
	Songs in a Strange Land	26
	Hope that Glimmers	27
	What I Hope	28
	Evening Psalm	29
	Moonrise	30
	Chiaroscuro	31
	Night Watch	32
	Sorrow	34
	Quarantine	35
Part II	**Through Shadow**	
	Halos	38
	Immersion	39
	A Prayer Like Lace	41
	My Father's Notes	42
	When Your Father Dies	43
	Emily's Virtues	44
	Metamorphosis	46
	Release	47
	Little Revelations	48
	Santa Fe Evening	49

PART III INTO LIGHT
  God's Big Hand 52
  A Wish in the Wind 53
  Seedheed 54
  Vegetable Patch 55
  Knitting the Fields 56
  April 57
  Spring on King Mountain 58
  Member, Remember 59
  May 60
  First Day of Summer 61
  Jam 62
  The Ripening 63
  A Simple Service 64
  Jesus Writes a Poem 65
  In the Beginning, A Word 66
  Some Poems Seem 67
  Kinship 68
  August Arrival 69
  Wings 70
  Bird Woman 71
  What to Listen For 72
  The Many, the One 73
  September 74
  Country Road 75
  Leaving 76
  The Landscape Speaks 77
  To West Beach, Lummi Island 78
  In Praise of My Left Ankle 80
  There and Back 81
  Driving West 82
  The Pang of Recollection 83
  Reminders 84
  Old Stones 85
  Last Night's Rain 86
  Shaker Chair 87
  Sun Shawl 88
  Recovery 89
  Notes from a Sunday Sermon 90
  Sarah Laughs Again 92
  Parturition 93
  Day Book 94
  Plenitude 95

Acknowledgments 96

Foreword

In a recent issue of *National Geographic* I read the comment: "Hope lies in the very nature of travel." We have proven this true during the long, restricted years and months of the pandemic when we have had no idea when the darkness of anxiety and isolation will wane and the light of health and freedom return. My husband, John, and I live alone, and for safety's sake we've remained for a very long time masked and at arms-length from our friends, and our loving children, grandchildren and great-grandchildren, some of whom have grown up and still live near us in Bellingham, Washington, our hometown. It was as if the sun of love and companionship had been shut out.

I read recently, too, in a book review about the difficulty of living with restrictions, that "Days feel long and months feel short." This is the kind of disorientation that has infected us like a plague, during the uncertain epidemic. And while, during those days, it has been unwise for us to board a plane or a cruise ship, a proven way for us to vary the monotony of the house-bound, to feel free, no matter the season, was to jump in our Subaru Outback and explore the almost infinite variety of highways and byways around our home, just south of the Canadian border. We live in Whatcom County, Washington, just north of Skagit County. Both of these regions are dotted with mountains, lakes, delta flatlands and farmlands, and just west of our home is glorious, islanded Puget Sound. From our west-facing windows up on our hill we are blessed with displays of magnificent sunsets over Bellingham Bay.

In the fall and winter, our forest trees are bathed in cold, damp fogs from the ocean, until limbs and branches, like old ladies and gentlemen, wear coats of emerald mosses and ferns like rich vegetable fur. We pay close attention to the shifts and changes of each month. We notice how, as light slowly returns and the weather warms from winter to spring, twigs and buds on branches thicken incrementally and sprout their rudimentary leaves. Along our streets the tree branches begin to look like lace as they thicken with new growth. I am particularly excited to feel myself a part of this renewal (see "Spring on King Mountain," p. 58). The fresh greens of spring, so innocent and brave, are invitations for us to celebrate the resurgence in the cycle of natural life and light.

It's these ordinary details that speak to me. How, for instance, the sun, so welcome after a long, dark winter, encourages new growing, an emblem of our growth in God, in whom we live and move and have our being, and in whose light we grow and flourish. For those of us who have lived through so many years of human experience this is a lesson we can still learn and live into. All of our magnificent creation responds to the sun's encouraging light.

In spring, as that light grows, we notice the resurgence of the intrepid, homely beauty of flowers and roadside weeds, fresh from the Creator's mind, including dandelions (see "A Wish in the Wind," p. 53). Summer's heat and light promote the growth of saplings and the long grasses along the verges of the roads. The farmers' fields are rich with growing crops.

Driving south out of Bellingham, we frequently follow the curves and angles of Chuckanut Drive as it hugs the slopes of mountains along the coast, winding past farms and rocky inclines with oyster beds visible on the mud flats below. On these excursions I always carry my little camera, with its Leica lens, and sometimes, just through the open car window, I'm able to capture the incremental stages of growing vegetation. I'm fascinated with the details of the landscape, infinitely varied, changing with seasons. Each minor detail is for me a message, a glimpse of a fleeting angel, a creative word from God.

Foreword

Richard Rohr reminds us that "instead of seeing natural things as merely objects to be used, we must allow nature to enchant us." It brings us such delight to be part of this abundant beauty arriving, it seems, direct from the divine hand. And as we continue to drive, and the landscapes melt and flow around us, descriptive words and phrases form in my head, almost without effort. Each of them, I believe, are Spirit sent. I carry with me in my purse a small green notebook in which to jot words and phrases—placeholders for later expansion into a poem, a story, a brief essay. When I get home, I'm impatient to return to my computer and write, allowing the fragments to join and find their way forward into verses.

The word "angel" means "messenger," and the title poem of this book, "Angels Everywhere," presents the idea that what I often glimpse is a flicker of glancing light, as if a heavenly being is darting in and out of view, allowing me entry into a realm beyond the physical, experiential world—brief revelatory messages from somewhere beyond that I long to share with readers and friends.

I'm hoping that as you read these poems (aloud if possible, and each one more than once), something like Wordsworth's "intimations of immortality" will enliven your own perceptions of the world as you experience it. Maybe your own fleet of angels will show up with their messages of burgeoning light!

Angels Everywhere

Some days I notice angels everywhere,
light glancing through windows, flying
through window glass lightly as air.
A human ear shaped like a wing,
curiously curving to admit the flare
of sound, hints to me of angels listening
to my listening, even as I sing.
What is that vagrant cloud, glistening?
Often in the blue heaven a trail
of light from a plane to me appears
as a heavenly body playing up there
beyond my grasping. Or, the tail-
light of a highway truck sends a spark
like some twinkly being in the dark
trailing her glory robe in sight
of stationary watchers. Once, daylight,
and a sudden, surprising, newer view,
when over the marshy grass a winged flight
invites a vision—Gabriel, or a Great Blue?
But often, through my twilight's skylight
asterisks multiply like silver sand and, near to far,
I link myself again, each night with Oh!
One bright, angelic, particular star.

~ PART I ~
# Out of Darkness

Considerations

Like Job, I want to be called
by God to consider the behemoth,
the leviathan, and the ant. To go
with delight into the world's rich
amazements—details that demand
intense attention so that I begin to
feel what they feel.

Ponder is another verb for such
inspection, and introspection. It calls me
to reflect: What will happen now, as
question leads to questing?

In my journal kinetic shapes and sounds
flow off one page and across
another as more possibilities
leap to be considered.

I am called to write
deliberately, a river winding through
the lowlands, the marshes, listening for
the call of open ocean and tides that
rise and fall, like my energy. And here,
here, the river water is taking a rock
in stride in its determined way,
an admonition in how to be whole-hearted,
single-minded, not discouraged by
ancient silt that clogs a free flow.

Gaze

Begin with a singular focus, knocking,
entering an entity, carving your way
into essence, then coming away
with a fresh consciousness of worth.

Rock. Bare twig. Raindrop hanging
from the twig—a lens for landscape.
Shrunken leaf. Antler. Cat fur. It doesn't
matter. And nose. The invisible fragrance of
blue hyacinth filling the air
like thunder. *Now!*
So unambiguously itself, unfurling its sail
over heaven. Mere episode, invader
of consciousness, a print on memory.

Inhabit it and explore a fresh cosmology there.

Prey

I am considering
the house finch with his
sherbet-colored breast,

the same house finch that
feasts daily on the feeder
beyond the window.

Our tabby cat, intrepid
predator, crouches, foiled
by glass

curious

how is it
he can see but not
clutch and ingest

what is right there,
a toothsome meal of blood,
bone and feather?

And I, ravenous for
closeness with
the living God, struggle

for a mere taste of
what would feed
the gap in me, would fill it

with body and blood.

Bones

My lines of verse are bones. I scalp
and scrap over the words, sorting and
picking for tender remnants, for tempting
connective tissue. For traces of blood.

I am magpie. I am vulture, a predator
scavenging to put meat on a dream's ivory.

In the world's wildness I listen for whatever
carries truth, compels me to say, Stop. Don't go:
Hold only what signifies as plangent, resonant,
reliable. Discard the rest.

The Sense Of Language

Some words glint and glisten
like mother of pearl, or fresh
dew on grass.

I relish syllables you can roll around
with your tongue, tasting, swallowing,
thirsty for more.

Language caught in the air,
written down like peacock feathers,
woven.

Lyrics that hold enough wine
you can drink them, intoxicating.

Words to drown in
and come up, gasping.

Embryo

When a new poem begins to stir,
a fetus barely visible in the sonar
of your brain, you have learned to
wait for it, telling yourself what you
already know, that it will grow
a body, cell by cell until that huge
moment of release, of thrust into
the wide air, gasping for breath on
the page, howling with energy, ready
for whatever the world will ask of it.

I close my eyes, and there you still
lie there, crying aloud, letting
your demands be known for the
complicated business of living.

Questions in Time of Pestilence

These weird mornings and evenings ask us
questions we cannot bear to answer. Masks over
our faces show only the eyes. We smile, the curve of
the absurd shaping our lips hidden behind cloth,
custodial, but with the kind of mercy that impedes
our tainted breath. Though I think I know who you are,
I long for the reassurance of unguarded features,
your mouth with its secret ironies, its open amusement,
an expression I have learned to love, inviting me to
join in our mutual sense of the ludicrous.

On the sun-bleached beaches children build
sandcastles that have even less chance of surviving
than we. We've learned to gather close enough to appraise
the levels of stress, our bodies telling more
than we may admit, even to ourselves. On the sidewalk
I shy away from you. Caution is in the air as we try not to
breathe together. On Zoom we decode the messages
hidden within vocal inflections, our features
familiar enough to guess at veiled anxieties.

Do your arms ache like mine for the embrace of
friendship? Even the scent of your skin, the
muscle memory of my hands reaching for yours?
We feel as if even our thoughts have been redacted.
Someone has taken a magic marker to blot out our names,
our stories. The air around us is thick with suspicion.
Anxiety leaks from the pages of the daily paper.
"What next?" is the only question we can muster.
We've begun to think about the end of our bodies
and what does a soul do without a body to live in?
Our living candles are mere stubs with dark wicks
drowning in waxy pools of their own making.

Persistence

We swim in a sea of isolation
blind among the waves, unknowing.

The raw fog, air thick with salt,
our skin slick as a seal's sides.

Stroke the next and the next, leaving
behind your rippled signature.

We have heard rumors of a sun,
somewhere above, beyond the borders

of plague fatigue. Move on towards
whatever light filters down.

Its calling. Its calling. Its calling.

Voyage

The open boat of
a poem
moves soundlessly
across the page,
its words, passengers
crowded together
on parallel thwarts,
plying its syllables
like oars.

Diurnal

Like a knife, early sunlight cuts
across the fields. The grassy
verges wake with a start, transfixed.

Hours later, walking, we touch the feet
of shadows as they crowd into a gloom.
And then, the unseemly rain.

Writing poems is like leaping
from stone to stone across
a river in full flood.

The best you can do is keep going
until the thing stops from exhaustion,
or you reach the other bank.

Enabled

Often, when I find myself unsettled,
caught off balance, my logic muddled
as water in a frog pond,

when my stance is
lily-pad unstable underfoot,
it is then I am enabled to investigate
the underside of the obvious,

encouraged to search out
the secret, interior colors of a geode,
sing praise for the aquamarine glow
within an ice cave,

and envision, in the center of a seed,
the radical promises of growing,

invited to shiver with expectation
at the uprising of sap in a tree's heart,
joined in the living forest's
unspoken psalms.

Songs in a Strange Land

How shall we sing the Lord's songs
in a strange land? The old rhythms,
the melodies of praise, strangle
in our throats and the words
fall to the ground like rain.
The air thickens with suspicion and doubt
and who's to say, anymore, what
is true enough to last, to prevail?

Isolation feels like a punishment
for offenses we never performed.

But let us trust, now, the ground under
our feet—that which has proven steady
for generations. Look up. The heavens
are still there, unclouded, beatific.
We breathe, even though masks clothe
our faces. Prayer surrounds us, close
as our skin, weaving for us garments of
trust and solace. Even in our isolation
we are joined in love, never alone.

Hope that Glimmers

The absurdity of a world
on its knees, whose fingers, even,
may be traitors and whose breath
may breed death. Its command:
"Stay away!" is the ultimate act
of friendship.

At the bottom of the well,
hope shines small,
but if we stay alert, head over edge,
we may see the water shimmer
with possibility.

At noon a pale sun glances.
How to begin to heal, believing
the world will not die, but live on
for us to tell the old stories
to our grandchildren.

What I Hope

To build a house of words
so compact and powerful, up there
on the hill, so sturdy
only a span of centuries will
wear it away, or crumble it, and then
only a few pebbles at a time.

Maybe a bell tower. Even before
it is finished the plangent songs of
metal struck by a bronze clapper.

All the while looking long and
deeply into divine mysteries,
understanding that verity may
unfold, showing itself in
the unlikely way a bud on
the chestnut tree's rough brown branch
bursts into an intricate froth
of white blossoms.

Evening Psalm

Though my fingers are branches
twisted by seasons of cold weather, by age,
this evening, resting, I lie back, arms
akimbo, elbows extended like wings,
though flight is never an option.

How good it would be to float,
to release the night's anxieties,
the restless legs, the heartburn.
A kind of perfection,
nothing needed or required.
Held aloft in the arms of the Almighty.

Moonrise

The moon comes up low,
copper, bent as a penny
left on the train tracks.

Like a chipped dinner plate,
or pale wafer, consecrated and
split in the priest's fingers.

You can't crack a moon or
see beyond its edge—
this trick of light played
by the sun.

And when I reflect back
just the bright half of me,
how will you guess
my shadow side?

Chiaroscuro

Midnight and moonlight. On the side of
the old house, a dusky constellation—
clustered shadows of unseen trees.
Through the woodland's tangled branches
the moon is painting the night on this ancient canvas.

Illumination speaks of light, but also of
deep dark, the painters' *chiaroscuro*,
clear/obscure, revealed/hidden. Color
bleached away, shape and shade speaking
their vibrant, primitive language.

Night Watch

Evening has fallen
like a cloak on the roof,
over the neighborhood,
but even the thinnest
rind of moon turns
my ordinary town into
a magical landscape.

Down the hill a stoplight
gleams red, then green.
The reflections of
headlights move
across the ceiling.

Middle of the night,
I still lie awake pondering
the mysteries.
I try to read the plot
of night like a book,
turning the pages softly
with little effort.

My bedmate stirs in
his sleep. Then stills.

Fingers of frost surge
up the window glass,
sharp and secret.

The room fills with
whispers, as if some
angel, some kindly
presence is offering me
the gift of slumber.

Sorrow

How granular they feel—grief and regret, arriving, as they do,
in the sharp particularities of distress. Inserting themselves—
cunning, intricate, subversive—into our discourse.

In the long night, grievances seem to multiply, old dreams
mingle with new. Disappointment and regret bludgeon
the soul, your best imaginings bruised, your hopes ragged.

Yet wait, watch. From the skylight the room is filling with
soft early sun, slowly sifting its light on the bed, on your head,
a shower of fine particles. How welcome. And how reliable.

Quarantine

After a long, restless night, the sun
brightens the curtains and once again your life
seems possible. Still you feel
blue, under the weather, even though you
have just admitted its loveliness.
Your good friend calls you and initiates
a virtual conversation that moves beyond
the trivial. We live in our separate houses
in our separate towns, but we ache for a
particular sense of connection, like what
Jesus meant when he said *Love One Another*.

How easy it would be to write
a note to your granddaughter who
struggles with distance learning. And when
the political news threatens to infuriate
and it feels like there's so little we can
do about it, let us speak love unreservedly,
singing, letting light spill out of our protected
lives even in the face of dark threats.
Even though we feel useless. Even though
we're exhausted—even then, let enough hope
spring up within us to spill out into the world.

~ Part II ~
Through Shadow

Halos

She tells me she sees the halos around streetlamps
as heavenly beings.
Shafts of colored light streaking from cathedral windows
do the same for me. In fact, any light works
a magic that some would call imagination.

Longing to see any territory clearly, though my old
eyes play visionary tricks, I call these impressions
good light. Or, better, God light. As though
the Holy One's persistence is enough to convince me
God shines through any portal in the world.
If only I would take the time, some quiet moment,
to shift my focus from a printed page to what it tells.
Especially, perhaps, one that speaks truths about
some radiance, past, present, and eternal,
that Julian might have called showings.

So, show me more. Enlighten me, You who are
light beyond night, beyond daylight.

Immersion
Lake Muskoka, Ontario, Canada, 1942

You are young, a teen with an
ardent spirit. This transaction will feel
almost as radical as a heart transplant.

Someone prays, then urges you on,
holds your hand.

The lake is mirror calm.
At the brink, under your bare feet, the pebbles
grind and sharpen your step ahead,
into this new arena.

The water's ice cold, but your resolve
carries you in, ankle deep now, while
friends on the bank sing you into what's next.

Waist-deep, and the wide lake grips you in its
chill welcome. Wholly. Holy.

You step deeper into the embrace of
the spacious family of God, into this
new medium that will complete in you
its miracle of decision. You know God
is with you, in you.

The level rises. Neck. Mouth. Eyes.
Your hair floats, loose as lake weed.
Heart pounding, breath held, you look up
from under. Above you, the surface glimmers

pale, a second sky. And now, above you,
it has begun to rain—small explosions of drops,
cells of dark liquid pattern the surface above you,
like eyes viewing the new you.

Above you someone is speaking words
you already know, about this small death,
this bright resuscitation. You open yourself,
and with a burst of energy are lifted into air.
You breathe, deep. On the shore people are
singing you into love and kinship.
The clouds have moved on. God's sun
shines on you, warm as a fresh garment.

A Prayer Like Lace

Sometimes a prayer feels like the fresh
smell rising from the lace my mother
had crocheted along the edges of a linen
handkerchief, like the one she'd always
carry in her sleeve.

In church, when we were young, to hush
our restless whispering, she'd draw it
from its hiding place and let us sniff
the perfume she'd sprinkled on it earlier.

I did the same when my own young
churchgoers fidgeted. Since then,
Eau de Cologne has always seemed to me
the odor of sanctity, a reminder to
listen quietly as if God speaks his psalms
in scent with words like lace.

My Father's Notes

A sample of his precise yet nearly
indecipherable handwriting, black and
angular as ants on a line—lives on
in a folder in my office drawer.
Sixty years on, it pierces
me with grief and love, even now.

She was the only one who could interpret
the brief, daily letters, the ones he mailed
from wherever he was traveling, loving
acts of ink on paper to her, the difficult,
needy woman he'd married.
The woman who was my mother.

He preached wherever he was invited,
his sermon notes on cards the size
of the handkerchief he carried in
his suit pocket. Minuscule, brief, pungent,
about the book of Romans, and God
and the victorious life (which he lived
to the limit, in a way I never could).

But the lines of writing, so precise, private
and inscrutable—I've saved them to decode,
in remembrance. I read them again on
the fly leaves of books of poems he gave me,
the little hieroglyphic: "To my darling daughter,
with love, Daddy."

When Your Father Dies

When he was dying (too soon,
eighty-three, cancer), my children
were very young, but I flew north across
the border to help him write goodbye letters
to his friends around the globe.

His ending took weeks, but every day
he'd tell me how full he was with joy,
with excited anticipation for his future
with God, like a boy (he told me) expecting
a new bicycle. In the end, very early
one morning, alone in his hospital room,
he woke, called the nurse, whispered,
"It's time!" and his last breath
lifted him up and away to heaven.

Emily's Virtues
Remembering my mother-in-law

Before her fingers lost
their cunning,
we'd shell peas together,
culled from her yard,
our thumbnails
splitting the pods along
their green seams,
releasing pale pearls
into an old enamel bowl,
the metallic *thunk*
a reward for the ultimate
virtue of diligence.

Another—thrift, her
unraveling and re-knitting
of old sweaters. Her baking
into fresh bread my child's
leftover cereal.

In her late
nineties, withered skin
yellow as old linen,
and her memory
slipping, she'd wake at
midnight, put on hat and
gloves, come down one
stair at a time, for church.

We'd lead her back
to bed, wishing we had
her resolve, her faith
implicit that the way she
honored God, God would
honor her. Would hold on
to her the way she held
the banister, tight all the way
down, which was for her,
the way up.

Metamorphosis
In memory of Virginia Hoyte

What fresh wisp of grace rises now
from my snuffed candle? In the shadowed air
a whorled gauze of smoke lifts
like a scarf for an angel.

Just a moment ago my simple breath
reached the flame, transmuted it
into a vapor that rises, still, coiling,
insubstantial, vanishing,

unrepeatable. It rises from the
black wick's death, a signature in the dark.
Is this how a prayer
shapes the air of heaven?

Release

When I leave
I want to be lit like a lantern
and then released, a mere wisp, no sound,
no fury, my small candle flame lifting like
a petal, simply joining a million others
some place where we'll never be
blown out.

Little Revelations

Perhaps we should consider stars as
outposts of heaven. But right here, on our own
lovely planet, flickers of early light
glance in a bright air along the morning highway
compelling response. At the stop light I write
an answer, a scribbled line for a new poem.
It starts to rain. I notice the way a single
drop on a windshield magnifies the whole
landscape. Look close. In this bead
a book of revelation.

And then remember how we, when walking in winter
beside a frozen stream, listened intently for
the flowing, hidden, underneath, singing—
the changing song of water under ice that
tells us what fluidity sounds like: The wash,
and wash, and wash of river water over stones,
each repeat fluid, a unique rehearsal for
the one that will come next. And next . . .

Santa Fe Evening

That night I watched a mountain
swallow the sun like a peach—
a hammered copper disc so large, so close
I felt warmed, as if a mother's hand
touched the skin of my face.

Watching it go was like singing a child
to sleep, expecting she'll wake
in the morning.

So much is beyond certainty or sight.
Yet when surrounded by fierce terrors—
anger particles that, unnoticed,
speed through us—
outrage, mortality, betrayal, intimations
of decline—we see beyond ourselves
the perennial marvels of heavenly bodies
that seem to hold us intact, confident that
we too will rise from our shadowed sleep.

~ Part III ~
Into Light

God's Big Hand

holds the universe
like an egg in
his palm, firmly, but
gently so as not
to drop or break it.

He covers you,
me, the universe,
each, all of us
at home in the egg,
waiting to be born
into something
golden as the
unbroken yolk.

Believe it, reassured.

A Wish in The Wind

The small child has been introduced to
a field outside the house, a field with
green grass almost as high as the child is high.
It is spring, and it has rained a lot which is why
the grass is so tall, and why dandelions have
proliferated with enough energy to cover
the field with a tablecloth of gold stars blowing
in the wind. And now, a week has passed and
the grass is more than waist-high and the
dandelions have moved on in their life cycle,
growing on the same stalks, and have transformed
themselves in the usual way which is also
something quite remarkable (which is why I'm
remarking on it now), and the child plucks one of
them and suggests to her father that they call it a
wishing flower because she has just sent several
wishes on the wind with the pale fluff that was once
a yellow flower. Which is why I wait in winter for
spring to arrive with its possibilities of dandelions.
And fluff.

Seedhead

Every day in the world
some plant fulfills its
eternal purpose, sending
a small juice of energy up its
stalk, feeding its burgeoning
seed with the seriousness of
survival.

The gossamer grass blade offers itself
to the green glory of the world
its holy vocation.

The gardener, in his need
to earn a weekly wage, ignores this
herbal generosity and, mowing it back
without remorse, extinguishes
its brave energy.

Friend of grass and flowers in
the wild, I am at cross-purposes,
paying for a lawn smooth as
a golf course while, expectant, I await
this new week when it will all grow
exuberantly deep and green again.

Vegetable Patch
"Rooted and grounded in love" —*Ephesians 3:17*

Spring, and we are flush with the energy
of hope. It's growing season again, and this week,
as I kneel in the soil next to a budding bulb,
or even my ancient, perennial rhubarb, I find
myself (and that word feels right: I find *my self*)
as if I were as rooted and perennial as this
living thing. When a minor underground upsurge
shows a flourish of green leaves and stalks
red as wine it's as if I too am bursting free
after a long, ice-bound winter.

Root is a word of promise, proof that life prepares
to thrust itself up into the light, carrying
the energy of hope. Jesus prefigured this
miracle of rising—telling us that only as a small,
dry seed dies will it thrust out its root tendril,
its declaration of intent to grow and thrive.

As those rhubarb stems yielded to the knife,
may I now yield to the harvesting hand that has
rooted me and lifts me from the earth.

Knitting the Fields

Spring, and the Skagit's new-plowed fields
are tapestried chocolate brown, their soil warm
and richly gleaming after rain, and sun,
and rain again. Row on furrowed row across
our fertile valley the farmers guide their combines,
over-turning the soil, patterning it for planting.

John at the wheel, we drive the roads that
transect this vital land. He steers, I knit a sweater
for a friend, an interior landscape of
variegated yarn that grows under my needles,
its serried rows almost the same rich color as
the furrows in the Spring sun. I knit a stitch
of red barn, purl another, dark as the wing of
a hawk overhead, then a knot the gray of a
fence post, a fleck the pale color of sheep.
Under my fingers the textures of the season
grow this garment into what I hope will be,
by Fall, rich and warm as earth under noon sun.

April

This day, this Spring-y day, I claim
the never-ending sky for ceiling,
and in the little rooms of my life
I cultivate seasons as if they are flowering vines,
growing across my bedspread,
and grapes, or seeds (promises for
July sleeping underground, waiting an
awakening, a green resurrection).

On all our ancient trees, rising sap
has thickened the twigs until they sprout
a thousand honey-colored catkins
heavy enough to swing in the wind,
flinging, in the bursts of wild air, their
lusty spores. And the cherry trees!
Exploding with their frothy pink blossoms!
Here is all joy, all gratitude, all grace.

Spring on King Mountain

Fourteenth of April, and
the pale scrim of young alders
radiates, lambent.

The deep wood holds its
bowl of lemon light, and each
sapling, every least vine, bursts
into leaves like green flames

I am akin, one of them, an old
branch aching for the surge of new
seed tassels, for a frolic in
the sun, for whatever makes
no sense but tingles. I crowd in
close enough to make it actual,
vivid, old words yielding
their own rising sap.

Member, Remember

I attend to what sticks in memory, anything
with a bright edge to it.

At the coffee shop, I can't help noticing
the young server's ubiquitous tattoos. My own are
still as dark and assertive as ever, twenty years
since that day in Vancouver. The dogwood
blossom still grows on my upper arm, paid for
in cash, its permanence a reassurance that God
made the dogwood and suggested I wear it.

May

Sometimes the year arrives so early it feels like
a lie, a false promise I long to be true. I cannot
keep pace with it. Yet I am infected, complicit.

Later, Spring is delivered in a lovely, long
gesture of descent, sun-filtered, agile.

Under the tendril clouds, the undergrowth is
tricked out with tassels, with sallow greens—
such exuberance and lack of restraint.

In the woods the generous hands of the big leaf maples
catch sunlight and send down their thousand
emerald wings, their gasps of brightness.

Buttercups crowd the verges, sunlight varnishing
their brilliant gold. Also the grasses, waist high,
like recently washed green hair.

And in the Skagit the farmers and their plows,
the fallow fields turning brown under the blades,
rich as promises.

I am next to a narrow stream where tangles of willow hair
genuflect, whispering, *This is the way the wind goes
in its invisible way.*

As the light flows so freely, without hindrance,
and as the creek runs into the river, so runs my soul
into thee, my Lord of all beauty.

First Day of Summer

We drive the cunning country lanes (that
seem to be, for no particular reason, circuitous),
between farmed fields, up a dirt road,
then out through the woods again, past a wooden
gate or two, then up to the foot of an abrupt hill,
investigating the territory from every
angle, determined not to miss a thing.

He drives slowly, patiently, while I, at my
open car window, scan the verges for roadside
weeds, so artistically arranged by God,
and glorious grasses, their pale seed-heads
bowing in the wind over the shadowy ditches.
The woods are filling up with lemon light. And oh,
over there is a little lake admiring its reflection.
The buttercups are over, but garlands of daisies,
almost as white as snow, claim the banks.

With my car window open, this first day
of summer, my camera's eye admires
and records it all with a frisson
of delight. Under the high sun at noon I snap
a distant field with cows grazing. My eyes
take a sip of a woodland freshet, seen flashing,
incandescent, through the lenses of leaves.
This world's greening glory will not be foiled,
lives on, cannot be held back. Memory dwells
on it, and these few words in the little notebook
I keep in the car door, ready for whatever's next.

Jam

Such a brief word for the sweetness that breeds
under the serrated strawberry leaves in the raised beds
strewn with straw. Dormant all winter, under snow.

But then, June, and you've learned to expect the white
florets to grow and swell until by some acts of magic,
and with a fine focus of intention, the pale berries

shape into themselves, garnishing their outer skin with small
seeds like jewels for a new generation. With the alchemy
of time and sun a scandalous red begins to show,

inviting the search and rescue of berries hidden from birds
but not from your clever fingers. You bend and pluck
until you've got a bowlful of glisten. Now the hot work

starts, the clipping away the stems, the chopping of
berries until your bowl is full of wounded fruit that
yields itself to the pan on the stove, the measured sugar,

the unstoppable boiling for the exact number of seconds
—an essential precision—steam rising, pink foam
skimmed off the top like a forgivable sin. You top up

the little sterilized jars set out on the counter like holy
vessels, until the lids seal. Later, there's always a part of me that
gets given away, my own heart the shape of a ripe berry.

The Ripening

With what enthusiasm
tomatoes mature on their vines,
yellow blossoms bursting into
miniature green globes that
swell through summer into fruit
plush as pin cushions, their weight
bending down the brave stems.

And the volunteers, the seeds from
last year's garden having fallen into
the richness of soil, respond before our eyes
to a new season, to the universal rhythm
of newborn fruiting.

My part is to embrace this generosity,
relieving the ripeness into a salad, a sauce,
a pizza, a stew, with an aftertaste that
reminds me of the Spirit's fruits,
a glowing, a giving, a sustenance
not constrained by seasons.

A Simple Service

The poet's job is to notice
and make notes.

To see with all the senses
so the words seethe with energy
until their spices
rise and fill the mind's
empty spaces with
fragrance and the
succulence of sound.

Simmer the ingredients, then,
until they blend, cook well,
flavoring the air.
Display them on the plate,
an edible work of art
for a famished friend or stranger.

Jesus Writes a Poem

When he says, *Eat this,*
handing his friends the chunk
of bread he'd just torn from
the common loaf, *It's my body,*
he's writing a new poem.

He pours red wine
from a jug on the table,
inviting them, and us: *Drink this,*
it's the blood from my own arteries.

A poem is made of metaphors: *this*
is that; those are these—emblems
and actualities both. So naked and
raw, these images. They invite us into
conversation with Jesus. Into our own
thirsty souls and famished bodies.

When we gather at the table he
provided—he the host—each of us
as guests may add our own responses
to this poem, this primal, imperishable,
nourishing, holy feast of Jesus' flesh
and blood, and we a part of his body.

In the Beginning, A Word

It is no sin to be in love
with language, from the Latin "lingua,"
meaning "tongue." If a word on a page,
a redolent phrase, glances up at you with
its open eyes, enticing the hungry mouth
of your mind, you may take its
honeyed crumb with your teeth and
tongue, and eat it as a word of God.

Some Poems Seem

Some poems begin by pulling in from
empty air syllables that seem to hang like
just-washed sheets and dishcloths on the line.
Wind fills them, shapes them in the sun.
The garments themselves beguile us with
crisp colors, the redolence of open air.

At the shore, waves crest and break in foam.
Clouds pile up and evaporate in the blue,
or cluster into storms that buffet our ears,
thundering, releasing rain, evaporating, gone.
Words, though, persevere on the page,
take shape and, when spoken into air, flow
curiously, fervent syllables sounding and
colliding with each other. Consonants
build like bricks. Unexpected rhythms
catch fire in the expectant ear, sparking
like bursts of electricity. This, then, is how
it seems to work, and why I love the words
that come to mind and write them down
for you, telling the curious way we live
our lives and write them into books.

Kinship

Sometimes it's close and immediate,
God's fresh air breathing into my lungs,
his eyes thrusting deep, through
bone and tissue, redirecting my own vision,
as though correcting some occluded
optic nerve for my clearer seeing. As well,
there's the ordinary fabric of thinking
with a mind beyond my own, that projects
ideas in colors so vivid I've not even
imagined them, and color-fast so they will
persist, won't wash away! The porous skin
of my soul welcomes his rain, a lather of
divine love. And then the aroma of
valley lilies breaks in through an open
window, suffusing and sufficient, as if we are
walking together in the woods in Spring.

Something so muscular and prescient
comes with connection, with presence,
with being God's kin. The umbilical cord
between us still attached, I'm tethered
like a child to his mother's hand while out
walking. And at the end of the day when I'm
thinking something utterly trivial and
mundane, I sometimes feel a heartbeat
of joy, a wink of fresh air, a fragrance
of presence for me to inhale, and release.

August Arrival
*for Bodhi
my great-grandson*

So, here you are, newborn one,
awake from your nine-month slumber
still wearing the garment of
sleep, soft as a cloud.

Families and friends
hush and lean and whisper
over your crib that is like
a small boat on this wide sea
of living, ready to launch
you, our fresh, small blessing
across the ocean of discovery.

To guide you,
we pray for clear skies
a good wind
and a readable chart.

Wings

I want birds to fly
in and out of my poems,
for a rhythm of wings
to move the air of my thinking
the way clouds of black birds
join each other—a swirl of dots
sky high across the horizon.

Sometimes syllables lift, words
taking off, drifting over the notebook page
and across the other side
like swallows taking the sky.

Bird Woman

Watching birds,
their simple, spacious lives,
(peck a seed here, sip a drop of dew
there). See them perched safely on a
power line with at least thirty close
relatives, with freedom to
fly when bored.

I want to be a bird woman,
satisfied with small, daily memos from
God who has promised food, and a
safe power line on which to find
footing in any weather.

Also, wings for realms I only
dream of, intimations of continents
to cross, nests to build.

What to Listen For

For too long you have stumbled along
the grass-lined forest track in the mist.
It is quiet enough for you to stop and listen deep,
almost hearing the leaves rotting in the mud
underfoot. You know you are being called
towards some far-away destination,
maybe a place of peace and celebration?

You lift your head and listen intently for some song,
some lighthearted melody, some reassuring polyphony.
Then, though you cannot see them,
above you the geese are sounding their throaty honk
as they fly a Vee towards their avian goal, the south
calling them so clearly, they cannot resist.

You lack wings, and a map, yet you have legs
that can stagger in search of the *something* that is true,
some music too compelling to resist, challenging you
to put one foot before another, step after step,
until you recognize, ahead beyond the fog, what is
pulling you, body and soul—what open door,
what host invites you in from the cold.

The Many, the One

The trees of evening are filled,
a sieve of leaves and small birds
with the resident choir offering
an evening orison.

But look! High on the power line
a single, sentinel robin conducts
the evening's benediction of western light
glittering across the bay between
the islands, all the way
to Canada.

September

The color of September shows up in
a certain ripeness of conclusion and dryness
of touch. Now, on the pale skin of recycled paper,
I print out what my fingers already know—
that shrinkage is tightening my hands like leaves,
veins prominent, knuckles white with work.

Summer already fading, out of the question. Light
arrives at an oblique angle. Scatters of rain. Yet here
we are, alive and attentive, as the bright tissues fall
from the sky with their brittle stems, arranging
themselves with an inherent art on the country road
where young children play, unknowing.

Country Road

Yesterday,
the singularity of a yellow
road sign: *Dead End*, gestured
us along the edge of the woods
to a quietude where gravel had
petered out and some parent
had mounted for their child
a basketball hoop.

It hangs there still, solitary,
ring sagging, showing rust.
Rotten strings dangle from it.
Father and child elsewhere,
playing different games.

Leaving

How dutifully, yet beatifically, Fall's
coppery leaves layer themselves on each other,
the earlier fallen having spread a first carpet
over the old, dry rug of gravel and October grass.
Steep hillsides around town grow flushed
with ruddy foliage, the first blush of the old leaves
on the vine maples. It all preaches how even
senescence may be a lovely thing.

Yet I cry about the losses, the inevitable decay,
and pray, with small remaining fragments of memory,
for my interior loves (like bossing my old wooden
writing desk with soft cloth until it gleams, smelling of oil),
showing respect for what is still an intimate part of
my life. And that what is yet to be borne in memory may be,
at least for now, sustained. But here, in this moment,
I yearn to learn the discipline of seeing something treasured,
watching it pass, then letting it go. Letting it go.

The Landscape Speaks
Fall 2020

A view will take its time to tell its truth,
but today, as we drive east over the pass
its fleeting canvas bares itself
boldly, for our delight.

At river-bend we park the car to watch
the thin branches of aspens undressing,
floating their tattered gold down
the ambient air, a few with every breath,
each wisp of wind. Again. Again.

Every weed and grass blade seems to
answer the season. On the highway verges
we tingle to the vine maples' ruddy flush,
the bright hands of the leaves joining
in mantles of ambient color against rock faces.

The white blooms on the Queen Anne's lace
have already turned in on themselves for winter,
their diminutive baskets of dark fibers
holding their seeds for next spring.

Under the bank the Methow mutters
over gravel, bends its pale river rush
down the valley. The land rinsed with rain,
intoxicated by sun. It feels too much to take in,
and never enough.

To West Beach, Lummi Island

You drive along the coast road
to the secret parting among the over-
grown bushes and vines to where
you can look down. You glimpse the start
of a worn thread of trail leading
down to the right. You cannot see
the water, or the beach edge.
Yet. But you know it is there,
the way you know a poem by heart.

Can you do it, your ankles weak
with the years? You know you must
begin, stepping down foot by cautious
foot into the sun-flecked shade, finding
spaces where your feet feel secure,
will not give way under you. There's a pungent
smell of crushed leaves. Brambles
thorn at your arms until you pull free.
Now a root makes a firm step. You scramble,
wondering how much further.

And now there's a drop-off where
heavy rain has washed the soil away and
someone has laid a board across it.
You step on it, balancing warily. Finally,
you're there, down onto the sun-warm beach,
welcome to clamber over the bleached logs,
crunching the pebbles underfoot down
to the edge where the tongues of little
waves lick in and out, wetting the stones
into their essential selves. Stones the colors
of clouds, but it's not raining, and you are
flooded with such warm delight that you'd
do it again. Now that you know you can.

In Praise of My Left Ankle

Oh, you who have held my
foot secure for every one of my
ninety-three years,

You who in my youth braved diving boards,
whose strong spring took me up until
gravity pulled me back down,

You who have worked so well
connecting my toes to
my shin,

How are you doing
now, now that the ground beneath you
seems like a series of stumbling
blocks placed deliberately
to challenge your locomotion?

I honor you, old joint, braced now
with a clever device for which I paid
far too much, but for which
I now offer my meager thanks.

There and Back

Between generous fields of ripe cranberries and
the gleam of corn stubble we drive toward the base of
Sumas Mountain, a crunch of gravel under the tires.
Roadside, the vine maples' copper glistens,
and by the bright brink of the road, Old Man's Beard
tangles with the peach and purple blackberry leaves.

Here, there, a grove of mighty oaks grab at the sky.
We stop and start and stop again on the dirt track beside trees
in full bronze leaf—like wings lifting in a sturdy wind—
my lens reaching from the car window to capture color
for the gray winter ahead. A sudden stutter, as a squadron
of spindrift blasts the windshield—the trees' un-leaving
echoing the ache of spent foliage, of our own leaf loss.

How the foothills leap and slope, lift and lower their
wooded shoulders dipping, dingle and dell! And how
the humble, ancient farms and collapsing barns nestle in
the gullies, settle into the grooves of their long remembering.

We admire apple trees whose boughs bend under
the weight of their rosy yield. Below them, the ground
simmers with bruised fruit. The ancient trees are left
standing for their slow sift into the soil of centuries,
their fruiting in old age a challenge for our own continuance.

Behind a split rail fence a white horse nickers.
A camera's click, click, and another click, and more
on the way home across the wide, alluvial flatlands.

Driving West

November's wind-stripped trees
signal vertically, their trunks gleaming
in a low sun.

Their nakedness reveals their lovely bones
doubled in the pools from
last night's rains.

With the woods, all the ground
is layered with generations of
old leaves.

How the tracing of weeds against
the low sun, spent in this dim sky season,
write the landscape with an unlikely art!

Rot happens, a slow sift into silt.
I ache to catch the gold
before it fades,

and in the lambent evening
the power lines above me display
their looping filaments of light.

The Pang of Recollection

Out driving in the Skagit. Sunday afternoon,
with a sharply-focused cold. A meander
along the sun-blessed valley, passing
fields of black cattle, stopping once to greet
two horses over their fence. We pause
to sketch a wooden barn, even older than
we are, green-mossed and back-broken,
now sinking into its own forgetfulness.
Old beauties are bittersweet, knowing they will
outlive us. Further on—a pond with its
skin of ice, the water-gleam in the ditches,
the rough field grasses' pale brass,
the roadside bushes and saplings, their stalks
still stark naked but splendid—wine-colored,
subtly golden, roseate, with minor promises
of buds. A bare beauty in waiting.

Around us the wide valley hunches its shoulders.
There, as for centuries, rise the peaks of
the Twin Sisters, austerely white with snow
against a sinless blue sky. The hills surround us,
like the embrace of intimate friends, reminding us
that though they are more ancient than we,
human ancients, we share the joys of seasons.

We stop, park the car, take photographs
to document our observations. Old enough to
remember, we know how change happens, has
happened us into an age of remembering.

Reminders

Things happen everywhere, at any
hour. Living is a moving picture.

I record this aspect, that view,
unique in its moment, fixed in place and time.
It will never be repeated.

In the west, clouds combed by wind, drift, serried.
On the power lines the black knots of
small birds line up like musical notes.

We bring each event, each impression
home with us for a second pleasure,
fixed in a film we rewind and view again.

Old Stones

In the bowl on the coffee table—
survivors from a Devonian
tropical sea, with what look like
eyelashes under the surface
—rest the remains of four coral fossils
found on the pebbled shore
in Petoskey, Michigan.

Also, a stone the color of a storm cloud,
and next to it another, dark, small as a thumb,
mottled with the minute white barbs
of (I'm guessing) bird teeth.

A chip of red marble from
the quarry in Caunes-Minervois,
the flush color of the ripe figs that
dropped and bled crimson on
the pavement under our tourist feet.

Others from among an infinity of
beach pebbles—slate, schist, granite,
quartz, agate—lifted from an island beach
just west across the strait
from my window.

I cradle each one in my left palm where it
begins to warm, as if asking me,
What took you so long?

Last Night's Rain

Last night's deluge
glitters in the farm furrows,
the roadside ditches.

Any pond with sun on it
does it for me. Any morning light
fills my cup to the brim
with a simple joy

that I carry with me on dark nights,
in dreams where flocks of white
geese glut on worms after
the night's downpour.

Shaker Chair

The transcendent intention of a
Shaker chair, shaped for a leanness,
a cleanness of body
and spirit.

How well the wood accepts the saw,
the plane, the sandpaper, the sheen of wax,
toward an ultimate rightness of design
and function and peaceful reflection. A kind of
lean contour that carves a space
in the mind.

An invitation for Christ to come
sit on it, or an angel, as Merton
suggested.

Sun Shawl

Early, I sit by the window.
The sun lays his bright cloak
across my shoulders.

All winter long I add
to daylight's warmth, knitting
prayer shawls for shut-ins—
knit three, purl three,
a kind of woolly trinitarian
meditation,

but nothing as golden as this.

Recovery

Is it better to dismiss a mistake
        than unravel
the whole cloth?

What if our aging
lives become unkempt,
        incoherent? Mere
husks?

How to turn a flaw into
momentum for
        re-inscribing it
           crisp, glowing with
a vivid array,

the kind I saw yesterday
        gleaming from a broken
glass shard
        lit by a low angle of sun?

Notes From a Sunday Sermon

So, here's old Abraham, his tent set up within
the cool hush of the Mamre oaks, whose giant, ancient
terebinths, older far than he, shelter him from
a desert's intense heat. Has he found perhaps a place
to listen to the old stories whispered by the leaves?

Then, noon, the day's most sweltering hour,
and a mirage, a shimmer of surprise as
three mystical figures approach his tent door.

Hospitality takes over. The ancient narrative
condenses a day's work into a blur of activity as
Abraham, centenarian, rushes from the tent, washes
the dust from the six traveling feet, invites the strangers
in for dinner, kills and butchers a calf, roasts it,
serves it garnished with fresh milk and butter, while
old Sarah kneads the salt of her unbelief with three cups
of her best flour and bakes it, a challenge under her
knotted fingers that continue to remember their skill.

The elderly host stands. Watches the three as they eat.
And then—astonished—hears their prediction (also
a declaration of fact for this old, childless couple) that
within a year they will have a son. A son! The sound
reaches into the tent like birdsong, tingling the ears of the
ancient woman as she peers from behind the tent flap.
She purses her thin lips in ironic mirth at this folly,
this impossibility. Her laughter sizzles like oil in a pan.

Pleasure? She asks, and then denies its possibility,
that the inconceivable could turn real. That she
might someday be known as a matriarch in Israel.

Well, Sarah had her son, and her pleasure, and not
a guilty one. May we now invite the divine energy into
our own sterile tents? Let us be open to surprise, believing
that the old blessings pass through the ancients to us.

Let not our old unbelief stifle the promise of fresh life
begotten, growing in us, no matter our age in years.

Sarah Laughs Again

She laughed twice, first in unbelief
and derision, half-hiding behind the tent door,
voicing the ironic tone of the skeptic.

Years later, more laughter, this time
of exhilaration, that God had not seen her
early disbelief as a barrier to fruitfulness.
That he had freshened her withered womb.

To conceive your first baby at 100 years old—
such an exceptional conception. It had
sounded implausible (and for it to happen,
old Abraham must have needed his own miracle).

After the birth we hope that our aged Sarah
had help with her newborn, learning
how to suckle a hungry baby boy from
those ancient breasts—milk for Isaac, that
child of promise, that offspring of her old age,

that son of laughter who, in the divine plan,
was the first of multitudes—as many as
the stars in the sky. As many as
the sand on the beaches.

Parturition

I have borne
a body of work
that has moved
within me, growing
a word at a time
from the quick spark
of conception,
into this creature
with fine bones
and hair the color of
fire, that I
labored with
and now see for the
first time, written
in ink on paper,
becoming its own self,
apart from me, leaving
a soft emptiness
where it formed
and grew.

Day Book

This day is a book still unfolding,
a suspense novel—we recognize the genre
(with clues from the morning paper).

We are beguiled by the headlines of
sun-struck clouds and dew wet enough
to rinse our hands in. The plot is original,
we can only guess how it will turn out.

We follow the narrative arc, reading it
through the burn and blaze of high noon
all the way to the last page until, like
an ancient writer, the night writes *finis*,
and the stars endorse the grateful author.

Plenitude

I sing a song of free abundances,
a bounty of orchard fruits, honey
for your tongue waiting sweetly
in its comb, flowers you hadn't noticed
drifting from an over-hanging branch,
buttered kernels on a cob of corn,
jeweled pomegranate seeds, the sweetness
as you bite into a fig, your cat's tongue's
rough caress, the hot sparks leaping
from an anvil, tributaries flowing from
a thousand springs, gems hidden
in a mother lode, your grandchild's damp
eager kisses, light from a far planet.
Grace, and Peace.

Acknowledgments

The Christian Century
"Angels Everywhere"
"Little Revelations"

CIVA Seen Journal
"Shaker Chair"

Image
"September"
"The Many, the One" (previously published as "General, Singular")

McMaster Divinity College
"Vegetable Patch"

Plainsongs
"Emily's Virtues"

Radix
"Emily's Virtues"

Saint Katherine Review
"There and Back" (previously published as "Driving, There and Back")
"Sun Shawl"

Saint Padern Institute
"When Your Last Parent Dies" (inspiration for "When Your Father Dies")
"Jesus Writes A New Poem"

Whale Road Review
"November"
"Country Road"
"In the Beginning, A Word"

With deep gratitude for the creative work of Jessica Schnepp in shaping this collection.

About Paraclete Press

PARACLETE PRESS is the publishing arm of the Cape Cod Benedictine community, the Community of Jesus. Presenting a full expression of Christian belief and practice, we reflect the ecumenical charism of the Community and its dedication to sacred music, the fine arts, and the written word.

SCAN TO READ MORE

Learn more about us at our website:
www.paracletepress.com or phone us toll-free at 1.800.451.5006

> "O that my words were written down!
> O that they were inscribed in a book!
> O that with an iron pen and with lead
> they were engraved on a rock forever!"
> —Job 19:23–24

Outcast and utterly alone, Job pours out his anguish to his Maker. From the depths of his pain, he reveals a trust in God's goodness that is stronger than his despair, giving humanity some of the most beautiful and poetic verses of all time. Paraclete's Iron Pen imprint is inspired by this spirit of unvarnished honesty and tenacious hope.

OTHER IRON PEN BOOKS

Almost Entirely, Jennifer Wallace

Astonishments, Anna Kamieńska

The Consequence of Moonlight, Sofia Starnes

Eye of the Beholder, Luci Shaw

Glory in the Margins, Nikki Grimes

Idiot Psalms, Scott Cairns

Still Pilgrim, Angela Alaimo O'Donnell

To Shatter Glass, Sister Sharon Hunter, CJ

Wing Over Wing, Julie Cadwallader Staub

You might also enjoy these by Luci Shaw...

The Generosity
Poems

ISBN 978-1-64060-514-5

Trade paperback | $20

"A profound generosity of attention, of vision, and of connection with other souls is what is most apparent in these epistles of the heart. Most moving to me is her candid appraisal of the human point of view, and her diligent watchfulness assists our own seeing, our own slow trek to what may yet await us, after the in-between."—Scott Cairns

Eye of the Beholder
Poems

ISBN 978-1-64060-085-0

Trade paperback | $19

"Luci Shaw crafts her poems in the way that she sees God's creation is crafted—seamlessly and with enviable freshness. Always honest with herself and her readers, she writes movingly about poetry and prayer and growing older. It is always a pleasure to spend time with her work."—Mark Jarman

Available at bookstores

Paraclete Press | 1-800-451-5006 | www.paracletepress.com

www.ingramcontent.com/pod-product-compliance
Lightning Source LLC
Chambersburg PA
CBHW010046090426
42735CB00020B/3402